Remember to Breathe

Holding On, Letting Go, and Learning to Live Again

Kay Barclay

Scripture marked KJV are from the King James Version. Public Domain.

Scripture marked NIV are from the Holy Bible, New International Version®, NIV® Copyright ©1973, 1978, 1984, 2011 by Biblica, Inc.® Used by permission. All rights reserved worldwide.

Scripture marked NKJV are from the New King James Version®. Copyright © 1982 by Thomas Nelson. Used by permission. All rights reserved.

Scripture marked NLT are from the Holy Bible, New Living Translation®, copyright © 1996, 2004, 2013, 2015 by Tyndale House Publishers, Inc. Used by permission. All rights reserved.

ISBN 979-8-218-73259-2

For Tyler, Landon, Blakely and Fallyn
her greatest treasures
In loving memory of your mother

May you always be true to yourselves,
find your strength in God,
and carry her love close to your hearts.

❧

Contents

A Letter to the Reader

We live in a dynamic and ever-changing world. We do not know what tomorrow brings. So, if you are hurting, know that seeking peace doesn't mean finding all the answers. Sometimes it just means finding the strength for the next breath.

The story that follows is an account of my journey to support my daughter, Jennifer, in her fight with cancer.

I'm not writing to you as someone who has "gotten over" grief or found some magical cure for loss. I'm writing as someone who is still walking this path, still carrying the hole in my heart that Jennifer's death left behind. The journey is lifelong.

Everyone walks this path differently. Some find strength in community, others in solitude. Some look to doctors and research for answers, others to faith and prayer. I found myself drawing from every source of hope available. There is no right or wrong way to love your child—no matter their age—through their battle with cancer, just as there is no right or wrong way to carry them in your heart after they're gone.

I've learned to walk forward even while carrying that emptiness—to choose strength and joy not because the pain is gone, but because love remains.

What I share is not a prescription for how you should feel or believe. These memories are simply the footprints of one parent's journey through the unthinkable—watching your child fight for their life, and then learning to live after losing them. I hope that somewhere in these pages, you might find a moment of recognition, a sense that you are not alone.

I would not have made it through it without God by my side. Someone once asked, "Aren't you angry with Him?" I replied, "How can I be angry with the one I am counting on to help me through this?" God was my truth, my anchor in the storm. Your anchor may look different, and that's as it should be.

If you are walking this path now—whether in the thick of treatment, in the quiet spaces between appointments, or in the aftermath of loss—know that your feelings, whatever they are, are valid. Your way of coping, your questions, your faith or lack thereof, your anger or acceptance—all of it is part of your unique journey through an experience that no parent should have to endure, yet too many of us do.

There is more to grief than any book can hold. What you'll find here is both story and reflection—my journey through loss woven together with what I've learned about healing. I share the parts that shaped me most, hoping they might offer some gentle guidance as you walk your own path. I've left others in the quiet corners of my heart—to keep close.

Remembering Jennifer

Jennifer was born June 19, 1983 and departed from this world on December 5, 2019. Jennifer was an amazing young woman who overcame adversity in her life—and made it her own. Some of those challenges could have easily derailed her dreams, but over time, she learned to view them as opportunities to grow stronger. Her path was not conventional, but Jennifer had a way of turning obstacles into motivation.

She had a remarkable gift for connecting with people of all ages. Her work circle included colleagues decades older than her. Women who could have been mentors became true friends, drawn to Jennifer's wisdom beyond her years and her infectious enthusiasm for life. As a single mom working full-time while attending college part-time to earn her bachelor's degree, she inspired friends to pursue their educational goals and reminded them it's never too late to achieve a dream. Her determination became a model for others, proving that persistence and hard work could overcome any obstacle.

Starting with a GED, she earned three associate degrees and, most important to her, a bachelor's degree. She built a fifteen-year career with Waco ISD, rising from secretary to a respected IT project specialist. Her passion, persistence, and resilience left a mark on far more lives than she ever realized. Jennifer's legacy will live on through the people who knew and loved her.

Being a good mother mattered deeply to her. She loved watching her sons' sporting events and had spontaneous song-and-dance moments with her little girls. Family was her heart.

In 2013, Jennifer found love again—something she never thought possible with her complicated life. She married in August of 2015, added two more children to her family, and was in the midst of building something beautiful...when life took an unexpected turn.

This is a snapshot of Jennifer before cancer entered our lives. The story that follows is the deeper truth—of how her faith and her love carried her through a journey no one should ever have to face.

The Cancer Diagnosis

My life seemed pretty normal, with its share of ups and downs—until the unthinkable happened.

I was driving to Home Depot to buy plants for my backyard garden when I got a call from my daughter. She spoke calmly, too calmly: "Momma, where are you?"

"I'm headed to Home Depot," I answered.

She asked me to call her back once I got home, but something about her stopped me—my words tumbled out, "That's okay. What is it?"

She hesitated just a second, "The doctor called—it's cancer." Jennifer had been waiting for biopsy results.

Everything around me stopped. I couldn't hear the cars passing by. I couldn't feel my hands on the steering wheel. I was numb. Somehow, I managed to pull my car into a parking space.

She kept talking, explaining that the doctor recommended surgery. This was February 2017. The rash on the right side of her tongue was a malignant tumor—squamous cell carcinoma.

This moment was the beginning of a nearly three-year battle filled with surgeries, treatments, and hospital stays. The cancer kept returning in different areas of her tongue and lymph nodes, each requiring more surgeries.

Each time, Jennifer faced cancer with courage and determination.

By June 2019, she was in the hospital more than she was at home. I was blessed to spend most of those days with her.

In mid-October 2019, her oncologists told us to stop treatment—it was no longer working.

Stop treatment.

We couldn't stop treatment because I knew what that meant. I wasn't ready to hear those words—let alone feel their full weight. I wasn't ready to let go. I was desperate.

Jennifer was calm on the outside, but I knew her mind was flooded with thoughts of her children—the ache in her heart knowing she might not get to watch them grow up.

And I couldn't help but think of her husband, suddenly facing single parenthood, carrying his own grief while trying to raise two little girls without their mother.

I told him that Jennifer would probably want to talk to him about what to do if she didn't make it. He gently replied, "She already has." She had told him to find love again—to remarry and not be alone. Knowing Jennifer, I'm certain she prayed for that kind of woman—someone who would love him and cherish her girls as her own.

As her mother, that conversation both broke and comforted me. It was so true to who Jennifer was—always thinking of others, even as her own world was slipping away. It reflected the depth of her love and selfless, generous spirit.

Grace Under Fire

During Jennifer's last couple of months at home, I watched her walk through the hardest part of her journey with sweetness and grace. She once told me she wasn't that strong—but every day, in a hundred quiet ways, she proved otherwise.

Jennifer was a woman of strength. She didn't begin this battle believing she was strong enough for what lay ahead, but she discovered her strength step by step, day by day—walking the path.

Have I not commanded you? Be strong and
courageous. Do not be afraid; do not be
discouraged, for the Lord your God will be with
you wherever you go. (Joshua 1:9 NIV)

She had many opportunities to simply give up—but giving up was never part of her vocabulary.

She had every reason to be angry, harsh, or impatient, but I never saw that in her. Even in the hardest moments, Jennifer was kind, sweet, and loving. Sometimes she would sit in my lap and hug me like she was still a little girl. Those are the hugs I remember and cherish the most.

As the cancer progressed, speaking became more difficult. Jennifer adapted with incredible grace—learning to communicate through simple sign language and using her eyes to convey her thoughts.

I remember one moment so clearly: her three-year-old was wearing a sparkly new princess dress, and as I helped her take it off, Jennifer danced her fingers in the air—playfully warning me with a smile not to get glitter on the floor.

When the treatments began to change her hair, Jennifer made a hard, but practical decision to cut it short, rather than watch it fall out a handful at a time. After she finished, she walked into the living room where her almost three-year-old was playing.

Little Blakely looked up, not startled or sad, and simply said, "Mommy, you are beautiful."

In that moment, through the eyes of a child, the truth was spoken: Cancer couldn't take away the beauty that was truly Jennifer, nor the pure, uncomplicated love of a child.

She still found joy in the everyday even as the physical challenges became overwhelming. Her face would light up when friends came to visit. For a while, she could forget about cancer—laughing over office gossip or the latest drama. It brought her back, if only briefly, to the life she once lived and loved.

Jennifer also loved her work and everything about technology. Resigning on October 31, 2019 was one of the hardest things she had to do. Cleaning out her office stirred emotions she hadn't expected. It was a turning point—a moment that reminded her that life, as she had known it, was changing in ways she could no longer control.

Yes, Jennifer loved her family, friends, and work, but above all, she loved the Lord. Her faith was strong and steady, even when the road was uncertain. She had many conversations with Him—some of which she shared with me, but most remained private, between the two of them.

Even as she carried these fears, she continued to draw strength from sources that were a reminder to have courage. The song "I Am a Warrior" became a source of strength. That choice says so much about who she was—someone who, even in her most vulnerable moments, chose to see herself as a fighter.

Still, one moment weighs on my heart.

Jennifer was sitting on the couch when she quietly said, "I'm afraid I'm going to die."

Without thinking, I quickly said, "You are not going to die."

Was it denial or hope that made me say those words? I wish I had responded differently. I wish I had paused. Maybe she would have shared more of what was in her heart if I had just listened.

I know she worried deeply about not being there for her children—her one-year-old, her three-year-old, and her teenagers. But I always wonder what else she might have needed to say. It was so difficult for her to talk about leaving them behind. Perhaps that was the moment when she was finally ready.

And I missed it. I chose hope over honesty, when maybe what she needed was someone to sit quietly with her in that fear.

By then, her body was so tired and frail. I sat next to her on the couch, looking at my beautiful daughter—so thin, her long blonde hair gone, her head too painful to hold up. Through tears, I whispered, "I wish I could take this from you."

She softly but firmly said, "Don't say that, this is temporary."

I often wonder what she meant. Did she believe she was going to be healed? Or did she somehow know that her time on earth was drawing to a close—and that soon, she would no longer need her scarred and broken earthly body?

The Wednesday before she passed, she spent much of the day in prayer. Her quiet place was her bedroom, kneeling at Grandma Joyce's chair. There, she poured out her heart—still seeking, still hoping, still grounded in her faith.

The Final Day

Thursday morning started like any other day during her illness. Jennifer had a treatment scheduled that afternoon. While we could see a change in her, she still wanted to go—and so she did.

After we returned home, Jennifer sat on the couch for a little while, then went into her bedroom. I went to her door and saw her kneeling in prayer. I stepped away quietly.

Later, Jennifer asked me to call her husband and have him come home. They talked for a while. Jennifer had decided to proceed with the doctor's recommendation to have a tracheostomy to help with breathing. Soon after, we called for an ambulance to take her to the hospital. After arriving at the hospital, everything changed. While it felt like an eternity in that hospital room, within about three hours, Jennifer's life on this earth ended.

Her life was cut too short for reasons beyond my ability to understand. But even in the heartbreak, I believe God saved her from further suffering.

Shortly after Jennifer passed, my son arrived at the hospital. I remember him walking toward me, and in that moment of overwhelming darkness, I felt rescued. I couldn't speak. I couldn't cry. I couldn't even pray. My body shook with grief. He didn't say anything—he just held me.

In that moment, when I felt completely shattered, he became the quiet strength that allowed me to hold on.

I don't remember if I ever told him how much it meant to me—that steady presence when my world had just come undone. I relive those moments occasionally, and still feel the same calming strength. I was drowning, and he didn't try to fix it—he just showed up. And that meant everything.

Grief silences everything—words, time, and even the air we breathe. Sometimes the most healing thing isn't what someone says, but the fact that they choose to stay beside you when there's nothing to say. Neil's presence was the only thing that didn't break in that moment. And that still stays with me.

Even in that grief-soaked room, reminders of Jennifer's spirit remained. My heart was breaking, yet in the midst of that emptiness, I found myself searching for something of her to hold onto. One thought stayed with me—"Today I Choose Joy."

My sister had given Jennifer a T-shirt with the words "Today I Choose Joy" printed on it. Jennifer didn't just wear that shirt—she embraced its truths. It became her truth. Even in the hardest moments, when her body was weak and the days were long, she held on to those words. It was a quiet choice—to cling to joy, even while facing the unknown.

Later that night, as I sat there with a broken heart, I finally found the words to pray. I asked God to bless all of those who knew and loved her, and to give them peace—and a healing heart—so that they too might one day find joy again, just as Jennifer had, even in the midst of her pain.

That prayer didn't take away the pain, but it opened a small door—one that would slowly lead toward a path forward.

Choose Joy!

Joy isn't happiness that depends on circumstances. It's something deeper—a choice to find meaning and beauty even when life is hard. It isn't the absence of pain—it's the presence of hope.

Jennifer taught me not to wait for things to get better—life will always be complicated. She showed me how to find a way to hold joy in the now—that hearts can break and still hold love. These weren't just words to her—they were how she chose to live, even in her darkest moments.

Grief doesn't disappear when someone we love passes. It shifts, stretches, and settles into the quiet corners of our lives. But even in those corners, we still find the love not lost, but a love to carry us forward.

In Jennifer's life—and even in her final moments—there was still purpose, still presence, still grace.

"Choose joy" wasn't just a phrase to her. It was her way of facing reality without letting it define her. And that became a lesson—not just for me, but for anyone who walks through suffering: Joy and grief can exist side by side. That faith can feel fragile, and still be real. And in that space between grief and joy, we find grace.

Jennifer's strength reminds me that healing doesn't mean forgetting. It means learning how to live again—even with a heart broken by love and reshaped by grace.

Choosing joy doesn't mean the path is easy—it means we keep walking forward, even with tears in our eyes.

Walking through Grief

I'm Not Always Okay

For the longest time after losing Jennifer, I was not okay. The words sat heavy and unspoken—until someone asked me, "How are you doing?" and I heard myself answer, "I'm fine."

I wasn't okay—some days blurred into night without my noticing. Sleep felt like a luxury I could no longer afford, and the world kept spinning while I stood still, watching everyone else live their normal lives as if nothing had changed.

I wasn't okay, and now I realize that was okay. Grief doesn't require permission to linger, and healing doesn't follow anyone's timeline but its own. Admitting I wasn't okay was the first honest thing I did since hearing Jennifer's words—*It's cancer.*

Maybe the real answer to "How are you doing?" isn't "fine" or "not okay"—maybe it's "I'm still finding my way."

That simple question—"How are you doing?"—carries so much weight when the answer is complicated by loss. Even now, years later, I understand why this question feels so hard for anyone walking through grief. It's not that we don't want to share our feelings—it's not that simple. The truth is fragile and sometimes impossible to put into words.

If you're in that place right now, I understand. When someone asks how you're doing, "fine" may be the only answer you can give—because the truth might break you in that moment, in that place. Sometimes, protecting others from the depth of your pain is simply part of surviving.

I know this because I lived it. For years, I carried the weight of loss in ways I never imagined possible.

There came a point when I began to wonder if I would ever smile again—if joy could return to a life so deeply altered by loss. I didn't know what healing would look like, or if it was even possible. And then—when I least expected it—life began to return, not as it was, but reshaped by grief and guided by a lost love.

Learning to Choose Joy

After losing Jennifer, choosing joy felt like a betrayal of her memory. How could I smile when she was gone?

16

Even more, how could I find happiness?

Grief wasn't unfamiliar—but the pain that followed losing Jennifer ran deeper than anything I'd ever known. The first few years felt heavy and quiet, as though life was happening around me while I moved through it slowly, carefully, holding on as best I could.

For the first time in my life, I understood loneliness. I had been divorced for many years, and Jennifer used to ask me, "How do you do it?" When I'd ask, "Do what?" she would say, "Be alone." I always replied confidently, "I may be alone, but I am not lonely." That changed.

Losing her completely changed my understanding of solitude—the space she filled in my life, even as my adult daughter, left an emptiness I hadn't realized could exist.

Yet slowly, through the fog of those consuming years of grief, I began to realize the joy I thought I'd lost hadn't disappeared—it had evolved. Not diminished, but changed into something deeper.

I realized that Jennifer wouldn't want my love for her to become a prison of unending sorrow. She would want me to laugh at funny memories, find beauty in sunrises and sunsets she'll never see, and embrace the life she fought so hard to keep.

Choosing joy doesn't mean I miss her less or that my grief has ended. It means I'm learning to feel both—the ache of her absence and the warmth of her love.

This journey of choosing joy while grieving is lived out one day at a time, one memory at a time. Some days the choice feels impossible. Other days it comes more naturally. But what remains constant is the daily presence of love—love that continues to flow even when its destination has changed.

The following poem captures how love persists in quiet moments, how we carry those we've lost with us.

I Thought of You Today

I thought of you today
but that is nothing new.
I thought about you yesterday
and days before that too.
I think of you in silence.
I often speak your name.
All I have are memories
and a picture in a frame.
Your memory is my keepsake
with which I'll never part.
God has you in His keeping
I hold you in my heart.
~Adapted from an anonymous poem

I used to think grief had an ending—that one day I would wake up and feel whole again. But I know now that grief doesn't end; it shifts. It becomes a part of you. You don't get over it—you learn to carry it. Some days, it's a whisper. Other days, it's a weight.

I may not always know what tomorrow looks like, but today I hold space for both—love and loss, sorrow and strength. *And maybe, for now, that's enough.*

I Can't See Tomorrow

The feeling of being unable to see tomorrow is normal after experiencing a loss. We choose to live so we get up every day, but the light is gone, our body barely moves, the air we breathe feels heavy, and our desire to do anything is nowhere to be found.

Remember to give yourself grace. We all move through this journey at a different pace—there is no timeline for healing. Don't be angry with yourself because you feel stuck. Take your time. That's okay. It is important to allow yourself time to grieve.

But having said that, if you are angry with yourself because you feel stuck, that might be your heart's way of saying it's ready to move forward. Humans by nature are survivors, and sometimes that frustration with being motionless is actually hope stirring within us.

When you feel even the smallest stirring to move, what might that look like? Deep within yourself, where do you normally find comfort or strength?

Start there.

If it is with God's Word, pray that He will speak to you and guide you—then open your Bible.

For some, it may be a connection with family or friends.

If that feels too big, start with something small. A text. A message. That small step may lead to a lunch. Or a walk.

If you're not ready to talk face-to-face, listening to inspirational music or audiobooks might be a good starting point. If you feel the need to express yourself—start a journal or maybe a blog or a letter to yourself. Sometimes, writing the words down helps you hear what your heart has been whispering all along.

During Jennifer's journey and her own search for peace, she stayed in the Word, but she also found strength from inspirational writing. One of her favorite authors was Max Lucado, a San Antonio pastor, known for his books about finding healing and clarity in life.

The path out of feeling lost isn't a straight line, and it doesn't happen overnight. Some days you'll take that step forward, and other days, you'll go right back to where you started. That's not failure—that's grief. It is simply part of the process.

Keep seeking what brings even the smallest measure of comfort or connection. Trust that your heart knows what it needs, even when your mind feels foggy and uncertain. Be gentle with yourself as you find your way—one small step at a time.

You don't have to see clearly what is ahead. You just have to be willing to take the next step—and breathe through today.

I will go before you and make the rough places smooth. (Isaiah 45:2 KJV)

We walk by faith, not by sight.
(2 Corinthians 5:7 NKJV)

I don't know what lies ahead. But I'm learning that sometimes faith is just the willingness to keep walking—one step at a time—even when the way forward isn't clear.

Finding Hope and Healing

The Pain

Unfortunately, we have to go through pain. There's no detour around grief, no easy button to press. The pain of watching your child fight cancer—and the deeper ache that follows when they're gone—can't be bypassed or rushed. It must be walked through, step by difficult step.

Healing takes time—more time than anyone prepares you for. It isn't a finish line you cross. Healing is ongoing and deeply personal. We each move through it at our own pace, in our own ways, with different needs. So give yourself grace. The timeline that works for others may not be yours. The milestones that mark progress for one grieving parent may look entirely different for another.

Some days, you'll feel like you're moving forward, taking baby steps toward something that might resemble life. Other days, the weight of missing them will knock you back to what feels like the very beginning. Both are part of healing. Both are normal. Both are allowed.

You will never "get over" the loss of your child. And you shouldn't expect yourself to.

In time, you learn to live with the loss—to carry it as part of who you've become. The hole in your heart may never fully heal, but somehow—impossible as it may seem—life does continue. That's just living—learning to breathe around the ache, finding moments of joy, discovering that love doesn't end when someone dies.

I am constantly reminded of Jennifer's strength and growing faith. She had a remarkable ability to see God's presence even in the darkest moments. When someone seemed surprised that our family made it through a particularly rough time, she would say with quiet confidence, "That's what God does—He shows up!"

And she was right. In the hospital rooms and sleepless nights, in the moments when we didn't think we could take another step, when the world felt impossibly empty—He showed up. Sometimes through the comfort of a friend's words, sometimes in the strength to get through another day when we were certain we had none left.

Hope isn't the belief that everything will return to the way it was—it is the faith that we are not alone in this journey, and that we will somehow find our way.

I came to understand something about grief. Sometimes we hold onto pain because it feels like our last connection to the person we've lost. When a colleague lost his wife suddenly, I watched him struggle with every decision, every milestone, every what if. At first, I didn't understand. But then I realized—feeling that grief kept her memory close. It gave him something to hold while he was processing his loss.

Healing doesn't ask us to let go of our connection to the person we've lost—but to carry it differently. And maybe that's where healing begins—not in leaving the pain behind, but in learning how to walk forward with it—step by step—as we begin to find our way again.

Finding Your Way

I hate to admit it, but I'm a control person. I try hard not to be, but I am. I used to approach situations wanting—and trying—to control what was happening and how it would turn out. But life isn't something you can control. No matter how hard you try, you cannot shape what happens next.

Facing the reality of Jennifer's diagnosis without the ability to control the outcome was one of the hardest things I've ever done. But I knew God was in control. I had to find the courage to surrender and let go of my fear...especially the fear that Jennifer wouldn't be healed.

Somewhere in the midst of all of this, I found peace in knowing that God had her—in His arms, held in ways I could not provide. What a precious gift—a peace deep within my soul.

That gift of peace became the foundation for everything that followed. It marked the beginning of finding my way through an impossible situation.

So how do we find hope and healing in the midst of such profound loss?

The answer isn't simple, and won't look the same for everyone. But maybe it begins with Jennifer's simple truth: God shows up.

Hope shows up.

Healing shows up—not to erase our pain or bring back what we've lost, but to walk with us through the storm.

Finding hope doesn't mean feeling hopeful every day.

Finding healing doesn't mean the wound stops hurting.

It means trusting that love continues. That your child's impact on this world doesn't end. That somehow, in ways we may never fully understand, their story—and yours—continues to unfold.

The hope and healing we find may look different than what we imagined, but they are real. They are gifts that come not in spite of our journey through cancer and loss, but because of the deep love that made the journey so hard.

These gifts arrive in unexpected moments—a memory that brings a smile instead of tears, a sudden sense of peace, a connection that reminds us we're not alone.

Holding on to hope honors not just our will to survive, but our children's legacy—their strength, their faith, and the knowing that this unbreakable bond still remains.

Life is beautiful—and can be unbearably hard. And somewhere between the beauty and the heartbreak, is the ordinary—that quiet place.

Breathe in the beauty.
Hold on through the pain.
And in the quiet in-between,
remember to breathe.

That is living.
That is finding your way.

When Strength Runs Thin

There are times when faith feels close and steady, and times when it feels fragile and uncertain. For me, faith didn't fade—not even in the hardest moments my daughter's illness. I didn't rage or walk away. But there were days when—watching her suffer, waiting on test results, facing one setback after another—the weight felt unbearable, and I struggled to find strength to keep going.

And yet, even in those moments of uncertainty, I was held. God's comfort doesn't depend on the strength of our faith—it rests in the strength of His love. I learned that He doesn't ask us to have strength for tomorrow's battles today. Instead, He gives us what we need when we need it—grace for this moment, strength for this step.

There may be times you feel a distance or disconnect—a kind of spiritual fog. But that doesn't mean you've lost your faith. Grief doesn't follow straight lines—and neither does spiritual healing.

In those quiet moments, I discovered that God's presence isn't a feeling—it's a promise. Even when prayers feel flat and faith feels fragile, He is near. The fog may be real, but it doesn't change the truth: We are held, we are loved, and we are never alone.

The weight of the diagnosis and everything that followed took its toll: the appointments, the treatments, the long days of waiting. It didn't just wear down my body and mind—it weakened the very core of my being.

I didn't see it right away. For a long time, the ache was all I knew. But in the stillness that followed, something began to stir within me—a slow and quiet recentering of my faith. Not loud or dramatic, but a deep stirring beneath the pain.

There were days I couldn't feel anything. Days when uncertainty settled in—a strange kind of normal—not welcomed, not comfortable, but the reality of each day. Yet even in the pain, I began to listen differently. And when I had nothing left to give, I began to receive.

I'll never forget the moment that shift began to happen. Sitting with Jennifer in their living room, I experienced something that forever changed my understanding of God's presence. As I watched my daughter fight for her life, I witnessed a connection with Him that I so desperately needed. I could feel His presence all around her. I sat quietly, unsure of what to say—until I realized I didn't have to. In that moment, I knew—God was holding her.

In that sacred space, a deep longing stirred within me for that same intimate communion. Though impossible to fully describe, it became a precious blessing—confirming that we are never alone in this journey.

It wasn't a single moment of clarity, but a thousand quiet ones. A whispered prayer. A verse at just the right time. The memory of Jennifer's own faith. Her strength. And somewhere in all that, my faith began to grow: Even when faith feels fragile, it is still faith. Even when we feel far away, God is still near—and He holds us close.

Jennifer would have loved to witness this part of my journey—the slow maturing of my faith. She had always wanted me to experience God as she had come to know Him, not just as an idea, but as a presence. She would have smiled to see me moving closer to Him.

God's Comfort

It is my prayer for everyone who reads through these pages that God speaks to you, holds you in His arms, and gives you comfort and peace.

There were countless nights when words felt inadequate—when the weight of grief seemed too heavy to carry alone. In those moments, I prayed a simple prayer, sometimes the only words I could manage:

Father, my heart is heavy. Take it from me. Let me rest so that my heart can heal. In Jesus' name. Amen

Some days this prayer was whispered through tears; other times, it was simply the cry of a heart too tired to form any other words.

God sustained me when my own strength failed. His comfort was real and present, even in the darkest of times.

Fear not, for I am with you; be not dismayed, for I am your God; I will strengthen you and help you; I will uphold you with my righteous right hand. (Isaiah 41:10 NIV)

This verse became a source of strength. Other scriptures would appear just when I needed them, even when I didn't know what I was looking for until I read the words. Each one carried its own power, comfort, and reminder of God's presence and His love. We are not alone.

Philippians 4:13, especially, feels like it belongs to Jennifer: *I can do all things through Christ who strengthens me.* It reflects the woman she became— someone who faced the future not with fear, but with quiet strength and grace. She did not give up the fight until the very end, although I know she was tired and weak.

When the ambulance arrived at the house to transport her to the hospital, the EMT medics were already briefed on Jennifer's condition and were ready to help her onto the gurney, but Jennifer waved them back and told her husband, "I can do it." Even in that moment, Jennifer's strength and determination did not waver.

Scripture has a way of meeting us exactly where we are. When comfort feels distant and our strength is gone, God's Word offers something deeper—something steady. In our most broken moments, these words gently remind us that we are not alone.

I am leaving you with a gift—peace of mind and heart. And the peace I give is a gift the world cannot give. So don't be troubled or afraid. (John 14:27 NLT)

While I don't know Jennifer's exact prayers, the following prayer reflects her heart and her faith. It could easily have been her words:

Father, help me to keep my focus on You when the pain and hurt are overwhelming. Help me be faithful and see the good and blessings surrounding me. Please strengthen my mind, heart, and body—and heal me today. Amen.

In grief, God doesn't always calm the storm. But He anchors us within it. And over time—often without realizing it—we begin to heal. We begin to live again.

The Power of Telling
Our Stories

I didn't know when I started writing that it would lead me to forgive myself for things I could never make right with Jennifer. I thought I was simply recording her story—preserving her memory for her children and perhaps offering comfort to other families walking this path.

Putting my deepest regrets into written words became one of the most healing things I could do for my broken heart.

There are moments with Jennifer that I replay—conversations I wish I had handled differently, times when I spoke instead of staying quiet, when what she needed was someone to sit with her in her fear. For the longest time, I carried these regrets as reminders of the moments I fell short as her mother when she needed me most.

But something unexpected happened when I began to write about these moments. Writing that I wished I had responded differently when Jennifer said she was afraid to die didn't make the regret disappear—but it did something else. It opened the door to grace.

I realized I needed to give myself the same grace I would offer any other parent in my situation. Writing about my imperfections somehow opened space for forgiveness.

The process hasn't been easy. Reliving the past has been difficult and painful—many tears have been shed as I've typed these words. There are still memories I haven't fully explored, afraid of what I might find.

But here's what I've learned: stories have power—even when they include regrets and fears. As a parent, admitting the moments I wish I'd handled differently doesn't make me weaker; it creates connection. When I say, "I wish I had done that differently," I invite others to do the same. Remembering can be painful. Yet healing doesn't require us to be brave all at once—it simply asks us to begin.

There's something sacred about channeling your deepest pain into words that might comfort someone else in theirs. It becomes a form of testimony—not only of faith, but of the human capacity to love, to endure, and to choose joy even with a broken heart.

When we tell our stories, we're saying to someone else walking this impossible path: You are not alone. Your regrets don't disqualify you from being a good parent. Your fears are normal. *Your love was enough—even when it felt like it wasn't.*

Writing Jennifer's story has become another way to honor her memory and to turn our shared journey through cancer into something that might inspire other families facing the unthinkable.

I can't go back and make everything right with Jennifer. But I can offer my regrets, my missteps, and my imperfect love as a testament to what endures. Because love between a mother and child, deepened by faith and humbled by grief, isn't measured by perfect moments. It's measured by the willingness to show up, to hold on even when it's hard, to keep remembering, and to grow from what we've been through.

In that growth, I'm learning that healing doesn't erase the past—it reshapes it into something I can carry forward, with grace.

Jennifer's sons carry this truth in their hearts. They've grown into the kind of young men she would be proud of— grounded by her values, strong in their character and faith, and living proof that love endures beyond loss. Even in their grief, they continue to show the kindness and strength she instilled in them. We honor her by telling her story and knowing she'll be with us at every milestone: weddings, births, birthdays—never forgotten.

Her daughters—now six and nine—have been blessed with a new mommy—one I believe Jennifer prayed for. They are happy little girls. Though they no longer have the mother who gave them life, they have a mother who loves them as deeply as if they were her own. And that, I believe, is the love Jennifer longed to see carried forward.

Jennifer used to sing along with me to a little rhyme about "a bushel and a peck and a hug around the neck." Now I say it with her girls. In those simple words, love continues—passed down, carried forward, never ending.

If you're walking this journey, consider the quiet power of telling your own story—whether through writing or simply sharing with someone you trust. If you're carrying untold stories, regrets that linger, or love that aches to be remembered—know that your words matter. They don't have to be polished or profound—just yours.

Your regrets don't diminish your love. Your fears don't erase your strength. And your willingness to be honest about the hard parts might be exactly what someone else needs to hear to feel less alone in their own journey.

Our loved ones live on not just in our perfect memories, but in the imperfect, grace-filled stories we share.

Sometimes the hardest

stories to tell

are the ones we carry closest to our hearts.

But when we speak them out loud,

or whisper them to a page,

they become bridges—

not just between us and

the past, but

between us and others still

searching for a way

through their own grief.

Living Forward

Jennifer's Continuing Legacy

A Classroom in Her Honor

In June 2020, six months after Jennifer's passing, the Waco ISD Technology Department and her beloved coworkers did something that took my breath away. They dedicated one of their technology classrooms to her memory—a tribute that honored not just her professional skills and dedication, but her heart.

Standing in that classroom during the dedication ceremony, I was overwhelmed. This wasn't just a nameplate on a wall—it was a deeply personal tribute to Jennifer's legacy. It honored the lives she touched and the colleagues she inspired. It felt complete—because it reflected not only what she did, but who she was.

The classroom now stands as a lasting reflection of the person Jennifer was—thoughtful, innovative, generous, and committed to helping others. It's a place where learning continues and her spirit quietly lives on.

For her children, this classroom is something tangible—a place they can visit and see their mother's name, knowing her life mattered—she made a difference.

The dedication also speaks to something Jennifer understood deeply—that our work, when done with love and purpose, becomes part of how we serve others. She empowered people to connect, learn, and grow, and that mission continues in the classroom that now bears her name, a powerful testament to a life well lived.

Finding Purpose in Pain

It has taken me time to realize that the pain—the journey I'm on—might one day help someone else. I needed space for my heart to begin healing before I could share the most intimate parts of this story. Grief doesn't go away. But over time, you can learn to carry it differently. You can learn how to keep walking forward.

The love survives. So how do you honor that love, remember that person, and still move forward?

Moving forward doesn't mean "moving on" or "getting over it"—because it's not that simple. It means learning to live with the grief as part of your story. It means accepting that life is forever changed—and that some relationships may change. It means waking up each day, holding on to what is true today, and choosing—day by day—to find your way forward.

I remember the first time someone told me, "You're so strong." I wanted to laugh—or cry. Strong? I was barely hanging on. But over time, I began to understand what those words meant. Strength wasn't about being unbreakable. It was about being broken—and still holding on. Still choosing to take the next step, even when it hurts.

There's a difference between surviving grief and finding purpose in it. For the longest time, I was simply trying to make it through the day. But somewhere along the way, I began to understand: Jennifer's courage, her strength, her love... they didn't have to end with her death. They had a purpose—and they could live on through me, those who loved her, and our journey of walking forward.

I can't point to a single moment when grief stopped being only about surviving and started becoming something more, but I do remember one evening, sitting quietly with Jennifer's girls, when the three-year-old looked at me and said through tears and her little body shaking, "I miss Mommy." In that moment, something in me changed. I froze, unsure how to respond. But I realized then—my purpose wasn't just to carry Jennifer's memory. It was to carry her love and spirit forward—to help answer the questions of a child grieving a love she barely had time to know.

The thought of strength has never come naturally to me. As a young girl, I leaned on my mother's strength while learning to navigate life without her.

And more recently, I cried out to God, asking Him to lend me His strength to survive the loss of Jennifer. I couldn't see how I would make it through the visitation. It felt more than I could bear. How could I possibly face so many people and greet them with grace when I was completely broken? How could I offer them comfort when I was drowning in grief myself?

But as Jennifer once said—when you are in need, *that's* when God shows up.

What I experienced was strength to get through the visitation and to keep moving forward.

Beginning to Live Again

If you're reading these words, chances are you're facing something you never wanted to face. Maybe you're in the thick of watching someone you love battle an illness, or perhaps you're navigating the aftermath of profound loss. Maybe you picked up this book because someone thought it might help, and you're not even sure you believe in help right now.

I understand the weight you're carrying, the questions that keep you awake at night, and the way grief can make you feel like you're drowning—even when you're surrounded by people who care.

This journey is hard. There's no way around that truth. The path through loss and grief isn't one you can navigate easily on your own, no matter how strong you are or how much faith you have. There will be days when getting out of bed feels impossible, when well-meaning friends say things that sting instead of comfort, and when you wonder if the pain ever goes away.

The way we heal is as unique as we are. What brought me comfort might not speak to your heart. The timeline of your grief won't match mine—or anyone else's. The way you honor your loved one, find meaning in the midst of pain, and begin to live again—these will be yours to discover, in your own time and in your own way.

So please—give yourself grace.

Grace for the days when you can't stop crying.

Grace for the moments when you feel guilty for laughing.

Grace for the times when your faith feels shaky and your hope feels thin.

Grace for not being who you used to be, because profound loss changes us in ways we never expected.

Jennifer used to say "Choose Joy"—not because joy comes easily in suffering, but because sometimes we have to make the intentional choice to look for light in the dark. It's a daily decision, sometimes a moment-by-moment one.

She also believed "Strength is a Choice." She knew courage isn't the absence of fear or pain—it's the decision to keep walking, showing up, and finding a way forward. It's choosing to face another day when everything in you wants to give up.

The road ahead may look nothing like the life you planned, but it can still hold meaning, purpose, and yes—even joy. Jennifer would want you to know that. She would want you to believe it, and to choose it—one day at a time.

So keep walking forward.

Remember to breathe.

And in that breath, remember you are not alone.

For Her Children

Jennifer's greatest fear wasn't death itself—it was leaving her children, especially her babies, who were so young they might not remember her. Blakely had just turned three, and Fallyn was soon to be one when Jennifer passed away. Tyler and Landon were older. While they understood there would be a life without her, they had no idea what it would feel like or how it would change them.

But reality soon set in. Everything began to change quickly. Our family as we knew it was forever changed by her absence. Landon moved to live with his biological father. The home they had all shared was sold because the memories there were too painful to bear, and Tyler came to live with me.

And yet, even in the midst of all this change, something beautiful has emerged. Tyler and Landon have grown into amazing young men—Jennifer would be incredibly proud. I've had the privilege of watching them mature. Both have chosen to follow Christ—something Jennifer would have treasured with all her heart. Her love continues to shape their character, guide their choices, and deepen their faith.

Blakely and Fallyn are beautiful, vibrant souls. At just eight years old, Blakely gave her life to Christ—so young, yet already carrying the quiet strength that so often reminds me of her mother. Fallyn is full of light and joy, and I truly believe she was born so Blakely wouldn't have to walk this journey alone. Their connection runs deep—a bond of sisterhood I pray will last a lifetime. It's beautiful—a wonder, and a gift.

I believe Jennifer's children will continue to carry forward the loving foundation she built so carefully—a love she held so closely to the very end.

And so, to all of us who loved her, let us be the keepers of her story. Let us carry her love forward—in the choices we make, the lives we touch, and the memories we share.

Keep telling her story. Remember to breathe. And keep walking forward—one step at a time—with faith, with grace, with strength. Carry the same enduring love that Jennifer gave so freely...a love that lives on in our hearts.

www.ingramcontent.com/pod-product-compliance
Lightning Source LLC
Chambersburg PA
CBHW020921140626
46545CB00015B/1156